That's Life

Life

**SOMETIMES YOU'RE
THE PIGEON,
SOMETIMES YOU'RE
THE STATUE**

*Quotes and quips
on being human*

Crombie Jardine
PUBLISHING LIMITED
Office 2, 3 Edgar Buildings
George Street, Bath, BA1 2FJ
www.crombiejardine.com
www.twitter.com/crombiejardine

First published in 2009 by Crombie Jardine Publishing Limited

ISBN 978-1-906051-44-0

For Ann

Designed by glensaville.com

Printed and bound in the UK

INTRODUCTION

Somewhere out there is a doctor with a sign up in his surgery saying, "Life's journey is not to arrive at the grave in a well-preserved body, but rather to skid in sideways, totally worn out, shouting, 'Holy cow… What a ride!'"

What a wonderful way of looking at life!

This is a collection of quotes and quips about life. Some are some wise words, others are just funny but all lean towards the doctor's skidding-into-the-grave philosophy: Life is a rollercoaster, come and enjoy the ride…

"

Any idiot can face a crisis. It's the day to day living that wears you out.

ANTON CHEKHOV

Adapt yourself to the things among which
your lot has been cast and love sincerely
the fellow creatures with whom destiny
has ordained that you shall live.

MARCUS AURELIUS

After silence, that which comes nearest
to expressing the inexpressible is music.

ALDOUS HUXLEY

A little sincerity is a dangerous thing, and
a great deal of it is absolutely fatal.

OSCAR WILDE

"

All sanity depends on this: that it should be a delight to feel heat strike the skin, a delight to stand upright, knowing the bones are moving easily under the flesh.

DORIS LESSING

All the world's a stage,
And all the men and women merely players.
They have their exits and their entrances,
And one man in his time plays many parts,
His acts being seven ages.

WILLIAM SHAKESPEARE

“

All truths are easy to understand
once they are discovered; the
point is to discover them.

GALILEO GALILEI

”

"

A man can be happy with any woman
as long as he does not love her.

OSCAR WILDE

"

And in the end, it's not the years in your life that count, it's the life in your years.

ABRAHAM LINCOLN

Anyone who lives within their means
suffers from a lack of imagination.

OSCAR WILDE

A pessimist sees the difficulty in every opportunity; an optimist sees the opportunity in every difficulty.

WINSTON CHURCHILL

"

Appreciation is a wonderful thing.
It makes what is excellent in
others belong to us as well.

VOLTAIRE

"

Arguments are to be avoided; they are
always vulgar and often convincing.

OSCAR WILDE

"

The art of living is more like wrestling than dancing, in so far as it stands ready against the accidental and the unforeseen, and is not apt to fall.

MARCUS AURELIUS

"

"

As long as I have a want, I have a
reason for living. Satisfaction is death.

GEORGE BERNARD SHAW

"

At the end of your life, you will never regret not having passed one more test, not winning one more verdict or not closing one more deal. You will regret time not spent with a husband, a friend, a child, or a parent.

BARBARA BUSH

The basis of optimism is sheer terror.

OSCAR WILDE

The beginning of knowledge is the discovery of something we do not understand.

FRANK HERBERT

The better part of one's life consists
of his friendships.

ABRAHAM LINCOLN

Better to remain silent and be thought a fool than to speak out and remove all doubt.

ABRAHAM LINCOLN

Be the change that you want to see in the world.

MAHATMA GANDHI

But what is happiness except the simple harmony
between a man and the life he leads?

ALBERT CAMUS

Choose a job you love and you will never
have to work a day in your life.

CONFUCIUS

Cowards die many times before their deaths;
the valiant never taste of death but once.

WILLIAM SHAKESPEARE

The difference between school and life?
In school, you're taught a lesson and
then given a test. In life, you're given
a test that teaches you a lesson.

TOM BODETT

Different men seek after happiness in different ways and by different means, and so make for themselves different modes of life and forms of government.

ARISTOTLE

"

Do not dwell in the past, do not dream
of the future, concentrate the mind
on the present moment.

BUDDHA

Don't be afraid to see what you see.

RONALD REAGAN

Dying is a very dull, dreary affair and my advice to you is to have nothing whatsoever to do with it.

W. SOMERSET MAUGHAM

Everybody's got to believe in something.
I believe I'll have another beer.

W. C. FIELDS

Everyone has a purpose in life.
Perhaps yours is watching television.

DAVID LETTERMAN

Everything that is really great and
inspiring is created by the individual
who can labour in freedom.

ALBERT EINSTEIN

Excess on occasion is exhilarating. It
prevents moderation from acquiring
the deadening effect of a habit.

W. SOMERSET MAUGHAM

Experience is not what happens to a
man; it is what a man does with
what happens to him.

ALDOUS HUXLEY

Experience is the name everyone
gives to their mistakes.

OSCAR WILDE

"

Experience teaches only the teachable.

ALDOUS HUXLEY

"

Faith is taking the first step even when
you don't see the whole staircase.

MARTIN LUTHER KING, JR.

"

Far better it is to dare mighty things… than
to rank with those poor spirits who neither
enjoy nor suffer much because they live
in the grey twilight that knows not
victory nor defeat.

THEODORE ROOSEVELT

"

Finish each day and be done with it.
You have done what you could; some
blunders and absurdities have crept in;
forget them as soon as you can.

RALPH WALDO EMERSON

"

The first requisite for the happiness of the
people is the abolition of religion.

KARL MARX

"

Getting money is not all a man's business:
to cultivate kindness is a valuable part
of the business of life.

SAMUEL JOHNSON

Go through the 'phone book. Call people and ask them to drive you to the airport. The ones who will drive you are your true friends. The rest aren't bad people; they're just acquaintances.

JAY LENO

"

The greatest lesson in life is to know that even fools are right sometimes.

WINSTON CHURCHILL

The greatest mistake you can make in life is
to be continually fearing you will make one.

ELBERT HUBBARD

The happiness of a man in this life does not consist in the absence but in the mastery of his passions.

ALFRED, LORD TENNYSON

Have no fear of perfection,
you'll never reach it.

SALVADOR DALI

"

He that waits upon fortune
is never sure of a dinner.

BENJAMIN FRANKLIN

"

"

Humour is just another defence
against the universe.

MEL BROOKS

"

I believe that one of life's greatest
risks is never daring to risk.

OPRAH WINFREY

I don't think of the past. The only thing
that matters is the everlasting present.

W. SOMERSET MAUGHAM

I dream of painting and then I paint my dream.

VINCENT VAN GOGH

If at first you don't succeed, try, try again. Then quit.
There's no point in being a damn fool about it.

W. C. FIELDS

I find it rather easy to portray a businessman.
Being bland, rather cruel and incompetent
comes naturally to me.

JOHN CLEESE

If life were fair, Dan Quayle would be making a living asking, "Do you want fries with that?"

JOHN CLEESE

If money is your hope for independence you will never have it. The only real security that a man will have in this world is a reserve of knowledge, experience, and ability.

HENRY FORD

If your morals make you dreary, depend
on it, they are wrong.

ROBERT LOUIS STEVENSON

"

I intend to live forever, or die trying.

GROUCHO MARX

I like living. I have sometimes been wildly, despairingly, acutely miserable, racked with sorrow, but through it all I still know quite certainly that just to be alive is a grand thing.

AGATHA CHRISTIE

Illusion is the first of all pleasures.

OSCAR WILDE

"

Imagination is more important than knowledge.

ALBERT EINSTEIN

In the attitude of silence the soul finds the path in a clearer light, and what is elusive and deceptive resolves itself into crystal clearness. Our life is a long and arduous quest after truth.

MAHATMA GANDHI

"

I saw the angel in the marble and I
carved until I set him free.

MICHELANGELO

"

I suppose that I shall have to die
beyond my means.

OSCAR WILDE
(upon being told the cost of an operation)

I think that God in creating Man somewhat
overestimated his ability.

OSCAR WILDE

It is a fine thing to establish one's own religion in one's heart, not to be dependent on tradition and second-hand ideals. Life will seem to you, later, not a lesser, but a greater thing.

D. H. LAWRENCE

It is a miracle that curiosity survives
formal education.

ALBERT EINSTEIN

"

It is a very sad thing that nowadays there
is so little useless information.

OSCAR WILDE

It is better to be a fool than to be dead.

ROBERT LOUIS STEVENSON

It is better to have a permanent income
than to be fascinating.

OSCAR WILDE

It is better to stay silent and look a fool
than speak and remove all doubt.

MARK TWAIN

It is not in giving life but in risking life that man is raised above the animal; that is why superiority has been accorded in humanity not to the sex that brings forth but to that which kills.

SIMONE DE BEAUVOIR

It is not length of life, but depth of life.

RALPH WALDO EMERSON

It is strange that the years teach us
patience; that the shorter our time,
the greater our capacity for waiting.

ELIZABETH TAYLOR

"

It is well that the Earth is round that
we do not see too far ahead.

MERYL STREEP

"

It's a funny thing about life; if you refuse to accept anything but the best, you very often get it.

W. SOMERSET MAUGHAM

"

It's not the men in my life that count,
it's the life in my men.

MAE WEST

It's true, hard work never killed anybody,
but I figure why take the chance?

RONALD REAGAN

Judge a man by his questions rather
than by his answers.

VOLTAIRE

Let us be grateful to people who make us happy; they are the charming gardeners who make our souls blossom.

MARCEL PROUST

Let yourself be open and life will be easier.
A spoon of salt in a glass of water makes
the water undrinkable. A spoon of salt
in a lake is almost unnoticed.

BUDDHA

Life is a long lesson in humility.

J. M. BARRIE

Life is a sexually transmitted disease.

R. D. LAING

Life is a sum of all your choices.

ALBERT CAMUS

Life is far too important a thing
ever to talk seriously about.

OSCAR WILDE

Life is just one damned thing after another.

ELBERT HUBBARD

Life is like a box of chocolates, you never know what you're gonna get.

FORREST GUMP

Life is not a 'brief candle'. It is a splendid torch
that I want to make burn as brightly as possible
before handing on to future generations.

GEORGE BERNARD SHAW

"

Life is not having been told that the man
has just waxed the floor.

OGDEN NASH

"

Life is pleasant. Death is peaceful.
It's the transition that's troublesome.

ISAAC ASIMOV

Life is rather like a tin of sardines;
we're all of us looking for the key.

ALAN BENNETT

"

Life is short. The sooner that a man begins
to enjoy his wealth, the better.

SAMUEL JOHNSON

"

Life is too short to work so hard.

VIVIEN LEIGH

Life is tough, and if you have the ability to laugh at it you have the ability to enjoy it.

SALMA HAYEK

"

Life is what happens to you while you
are making other plans.

JOHN LENNON

"

Life loves to be taken by the lapel and
told, "I am with you, kid! Let's go!"

MAYA ANGELOU

"

Life's greatest happiness is to be convinced we are loved.

VICTOR HUGO

,,

Live as if you were to die tomorrow.
Learn as if you were to live forever.

MAHATMA GANDHI

Live to the point of tears.

ALBERT CAMUS

The man who views the world at 50
the same as he did at 20 has
wasted 30 years of his life.

MUHAMMAD ALI

Men occasionally stumble over the truth,
but most of them pick themselves up and
hurry off as if nothing ever happened.

WINSTON CHURCHILL

Middle age is when you've met so many
people that every new person you
meet reminds you of someone else.

OGDEN NASH

Mistakes are the portals of discovery.

JAMES JOYCE

Mistrust the man who finds everything good, the man who finds everything evil and still more the man who is indifferent to everything.

JOHANN K. LAVATER

Morality is herd instinct in the individual.

FRIEDRICH NIETZSCHE

Most folks are about as happy as
they make up their minds to be.

ABRAHAM LINCOLN

Most modern calendars mar the sweet
simplicity of our lives by reminding us that
each day that passes is the anniversary
of some perfectly uninteresting event.

OSCAR WILDE

Music makes one feel so romantic, at least
it always gets on one's nerves – which
is the same thing nowadays.

OSCAR WILDE

"

My formula for living is quite simple. I get up in the morning and I go to bed at night. In between, I occupy myself as best I can.

CARY GRANT

Never interrupt your enemy when
he is making a mistake.

NAPOLEON BONAPARTE

Nurture your mind with great thoughts,
for you will never go any higher
than you think.

BENJAMIN DISRAELI

One of the advantages of being disorderly
is that one is constantly making
exciting discoveries.

A. A. MILNE

One of the keys to happiness is a bad memory.

RITA MAE BROWN

Opportunity is missed by most people because
it is dressed in overalls and looks like work.

THOMAS EDISON

Ordinary riches can be stolen: real riches cannot. In your soul are infinitely precious things that cannot be taken from you.

OSCAR WILDE

Our lives begin to end the day we
become silent about things that matter.

MARTIN LUTHER KING, JR.

People ask for criticism but they only want praise.

W. SOMERSET MAUGHAM

Remember, a dead fish can float downstream,
but it takes a live one to swim upstream.

W. C. FIELDS

"

Remember this, that very little is
needed to make a happy life.

MARCUS AURELIUS

"

The secret of life is honesty and fair dealing.
If you can fake that, you've got it made.

GROUCHO MARX

Avoiding danger is no safer in the long
run than outright exposure. Life is either
a daring adventure, or nothing.

HELEN KELLER

Seriousness is the only refuge of the shallow.

OSCAR WILDE

"

Sleep: the most beautiful experience in
life, except drink.

W. C. FIELDS

Start every day off with a smile and
get it over with.

W. C. FIELDS

Success is not final, failure is not fatal: it is the courage to continue that counts.

WINSTON CHURCHILL

Take care of the luxuries and the necessities
will take care of themselves.

DOROTHY PARKER

The important thing is not to stop questioning.
Curiosity has its own reason for existing.

ALBERT EINSTEIN

The only man who makes no mistakes is the man
who never does anything.

THEODORE ROOSEVELT

There are only two ways to live your life.
One is as though nothing is a miracle.
The other is as if everything is.

ALBERT EINSTEIN

There is no feeling, except the extremes
of fear and grief, that does not
find relief in music.

GEORGE ELIOT

Thomas Jefferson once said, 'We should never judge a president by his age, only by his works.' And ever since he told me that, I stopped worrying.

RONALD REAGAN

To be stupid, selfish, and have good health
are three requirements for happiness,
though if stupidity is lacking, all is lost.

GUSTAVE FLAUBERT

"

To know what you prefer instead of humbly saying
'Amen' to what the world tells you you ought
to prefer, is to have kept your soul alive.

ROBERT LOUIS STEVENSON

"

"

To live is like to love: all reason is against it,
and all healthy instinct for it.

SAMUEL BUTLER

"

The truth is rarely pure and never simple.

OSCAR WILDE

Twenty years from now you will be more disappointed by the things that you didn't do than by the ones you did do. So throw off the bowlines. Sail away from the safe harbour. Catch the trade winds in your sails. Explore. Dream. Discover.

MARK TWAIN

We do not receive wisdom,
we must discover it for ourselves,
after a journey through the wilderness
which no one else can make for us,
which no one can spare us,
for our wisdom is the point of view
from which we come at last
to regard the world.

MARCEL PROUST

"

We must be willing to let go of the life
we have planned, so as to have
the life that is waiting for us.

E. M. FORSTER

"

Whatever you do, you need courage.
Whatever course you decide upon, there is
always someone to tell you you are wrong.
There are always difficulties arising which
tempt you to believe that your critics are
right. To map out a course of action and
follow it to the end requires some of the
same courage which a soldier needs.

RALPH WALDO EMERSON

"

When life appears to be working against you,
when your luck is down, when the supposedly
wrong people show up, or when you slip up and
return to old, self-defeating habits, recognize the
signs that you're out of harmony with intention.

ALDOUS HUXLEY

When you come to a roadblock,
take a detour.

BARBARA BUSH

When written in Chinese, the word 'crisis' is composed of two characters. One represents danger and the other represents opportunity.

JOHN F. KENNEDY

Without friends, no one would want to live,
even if he had all other goods.

ARISTOTLE

"

You must be the change you wish
to see in the world.

MAHATMA GANDHI

"

You are only young once, but you can
stay immature indefinitely.

OGDEN NASH

You have enemies? Good. That means
you've stood up for something,
sometime in your life.

WINSTON CHURCHILL

You only live once, but if you do it right,
once is enough.

MAE WEST

You're never too old to become younger.

MAE WEST

"

Youthfulness is connected to the ability to see things new for the first time. So if your eyes still look at life with wonder, then you will seem young, even though you may not be chronologically young.

GOLDIE HAWN

"

You will never be happy if you continue to search
for what happiness consists of. You will never live
if you are looking for the meaning of life.

ALBERT CAMUS

INDEX OF NAMES